Contents

Some words are shown in bold, **like this.** You can find out what they mean by looking in the glossary.

Where is North America?

We divide the world into seven large areas of land called **continents**. You can see them on the map of the world below. North America is the third-largest continent in the world.

NORTH AMERICA

EUROPE

ASIA

ATLANTIC OCEAN

AFRICA

PACIFIC OCEAN

PACIFIC OCEAN

SOUTH AMERICA

INDIAN OCEAN

N
W · E
S

AUSTRALIA

ANTARCTICA

Can you see the continent of North America?

Animals in Danger

in North America

Louise and Richard Spilsbury

Raintree is an imprint of Capstone Global Library
Limited, a company incorporated in England and Wales
having its registered office at 7 Pilgrim Street, London,
EC4V 6LB – Registered company number: 6695582

www.raintreepublishers.co.uk
myorders@raintreepublishers.co.uk

Text © Capstone Global Library Limited 2013
First published in hardback in 2013
Paperback edition first published in 2014
The moral rights of the proprietor have been asserted.

Edited by Rebecca Rissman, Dan Nunn, and Adrian
Vigliano
Designed by Philippa Jenkins
Picture research by Tracy Cummins
Originated by Capstone Global Library Ltd
Printed in China by South China Printing Company Ltd

ISBN 978 1 406 26209 4 (hardback)
17 16 15 14 13
10 9 8 7 6 5 4 3 2 1

ISBN 978 1 406 26216 2 (paperback)
18 17 16 15 14
10 9 8 7 6 5 4 3 2 1

British Library Cataloguing in Publication Data
A full catalogue record for this book is available from
the British Library.

Acknowledgements
We would like to thank the following for permission to
reproduce photographs: Alamy pp. 13 (© Stone Nature
Photography), 25 (© Scott Camazine), 28 (© Design
Pics Inc.), 29 (© AR Photo); istockphoto pp. 11 (@ John
Pitcher), 19 (© Paul Tessier); National Geographic
Stock p. 17 (Joel Sartore); Photo Researchers, Inc. p.
6 (Richard R. Hansen); Shutterstock pp. 4 (© Chris P.),
5 bottom (© ArnaudS2), 5 top (© kavram), 10 (©
Yvonne Pijnenburg-Schonewille), 14 (© kojihirano),
21 (© Naaman Abreu), icons (© Florian Augustin), (©
tristan tan), maps (© AridOcean); Superstock pp. 9
(© James Urbach), 15 (© Design Pics), 18 (© Juniors),
22 (© Animals Animals), 23 (© Juniors), 26 (© Minden
Pictures), 27 (© NaturePL).

Cover photograph of a young polar bear reproduced
with permission of Shutterstock (© Peter Kirillov).
Cover photograph of Costa Rican American crocodile
reproduced with permission of Shutterstock (©
worldswildlifewonders).
Cover photograph of USA, California, Big Sur
reproduced with permission of Superstock (©
Exactostock).
Cover photograph of red wolf reproduced with
permission of Getty Images (Mark Conlin).

We would like to thank Michael Bright for his invaluable
help in the preparation of this book.

Every effort has been made to contact copyright
holders of any material reproduced in this book. Any
omissions will be rectified in subsequent printings if
notice is given to the publisher.

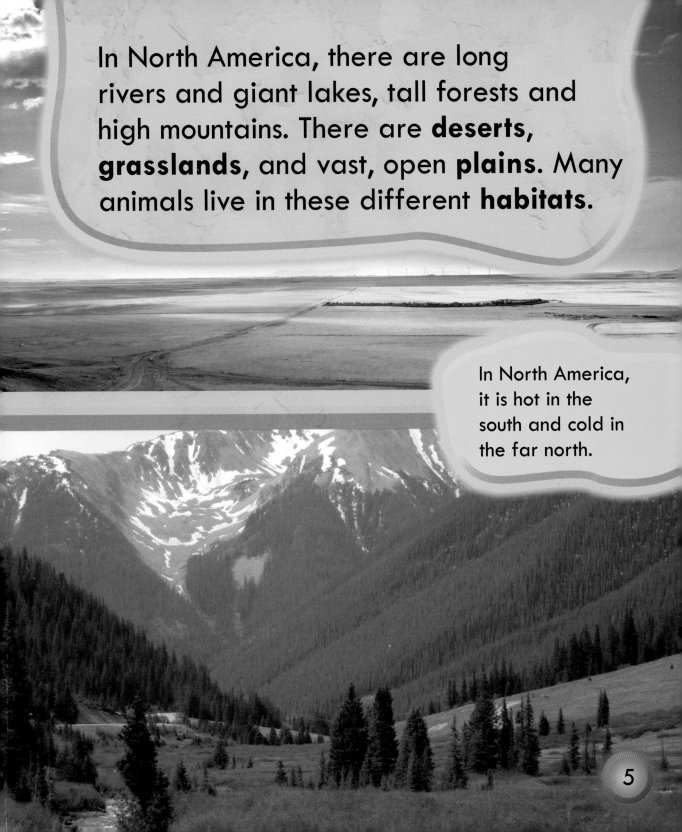

In North America, there are long rivers and giant lakes, tall forests and high mountains. There are **deserts, grasslands,** and vast, open **plains.** Many animals live in these different **habitats.**

In North America, it is hot in the south and cold in the far north.

5

Animals of North America

Some animals in North America are **endangered**. There are very few of that type of animal left. If they all die, that type of animal will be **extinct**. Animals that are extinct are gone from the planet forever.

The giant kangaroo rat is one of North America's endangered animals.

Different types of animals look and behave differently from each other. We sort them into groups to help tell them apart.

Animal classification chart

Amphibian	• lives on land and in water • has damp, smooth skin • has **webbed** feet • lays many eggs	
Bird	• has feathers and wings • hatches out of hard-shelled eggs	
Fish	• lives in water • has **fins** and most have **scales** • young hatch from soft eggs	
Mammal	• drinks milk when a baby • has hair on its body	
Reptile	• has scales on its body • lives on land • young hatch from soft-shelled eggs	

Look out for pictures like these next to each photo. They will tell you what type of animal each photo shows.

Canada and Alaska

There are vast areas of snow and ice in Canada and Alaska, and forests of pine and fir trees with areas of **wetlands**. People use many of these areas to build or farm on.

ARCTIC OCEAN

BROOKS RANGE

MACKENZIE MOUNTAINS

Mackenzie River

Yukon River

ALASKA RANGE

ROCKY MOUNTAINS

Saskatchewan River

PACIFIC OCEAN

ATLANTIC OCEAN

N
W E
S

This map shows Canada and Alaska.

Whooping cranes got their name from their whooping cry. They eat crabs, fish, frogs, and other **prey** from wetlands. They make nests from mud and plants in wetlands to keep eggs safe from **predators.**

At 1.5 metres (5 feet) high, these cranes are the tallest birds in North America.

To keep them warm, polar bears have a layer of fat 10 centimetres thick.

The polar bear travels long distances to find prey, often drifting on blocks of floating ice. It hunts for seals by waiting for them to appear at breathing holes in the ice. **Global warming** melts the ice and stops polar bears from finding food.

Walruses need to rest on ice platforms, too. Then they dive to catch clams, crabs, and other animals to eat. They have 600 whiskers around their mouth that feel along the sea floor for prey.

The walrus uses its huge tusks to pull itself onto ice platforms to rest.

In the west

Some **endangered** animals in western North America live in **deserts**, mountains, and **scrubland**. Scrubland is dry land where few plants grow.

PACIFIC OCEAN

CASCADE MOUNTAINS

Columbia River

coastal forest

Great Basin Desert

Mojave Desert

Colorado River

ROCKY MOUNTAINS

Sonoran Desert

This map shows the western region of North America.

The Devil's Hole pupfish lives only in one deep, water-filled cave in the desert. It eats green **algae** from the rocks. It is in danger because people pumped water out of the cave to water farmland.

In real life, Devil's Hole pupfish are less than 25 millimetres (1 inch) long!

The California condor's wings stretch almost 3 metres (10 feet) from tip to tip! A condor flies high over rock and scrubland looking for dead animals to eat. Its bald head stops rotting food from sticking to it when eating!

Condors die from lead poisoning when they eat animals that were killed by lead bullets.

This lizard can leap up to 60 centimetres (2 feet) in the air to catch **prey**!

The blunt-nosed leopard lizard scurries across flat, dry land. It sleeps in other animals' burrows and hunts for grasshoppers and other **insects** by day. People take over its **habitat** for homes and farms.

15

Central and eastern states

Some **endangered** animals in central and eastern America live in **prairies**, lakes, and rivers. People dig up prairies for farmland. They build **dams** that make water in rivers and lakes colder and flow faster.

This is the central and eastern region of North America.

Lake Superior

Lake Huron

Lake Ontario

Lake Michigan

Lake Erie

Mississippi River

Missouri River

prairie

Ohio River

APPALACHIAN MOUNTAINS

ATLANTIC OCEAN

N
W   E
S

Young pallid sturgeons need areas of warm, slow water to feed and grow. Adults use their four long barbels to feel for small animals in the mud. Then their mouth sucks the food up fast, like a vacuum cleaner!

These sturgeons can grow to 2 metres (6 feet) long!

barbels

This ferret's large front paws have sharp claws for digging into burrows.

Black-footed ferrets have narrow bodies to squeeze into prairie dog burrows. They sleep during the day and hunt prairie dogs at night. With fewer prairies, there are fewer prairie dogs for them to eat.

Piping plovers eat worms and crabs. They lay eggs in shallow holes filled with stones near rivers and lakes. Chicks that hatch out of the eggs eat **insects** from the sand. Today, there is less space for plovers to nest.

The plover's sandy colour makes it harder for foxes and other **predators** to spot!

19

In the south

Animals in swamps and other **wetlands** in southern North America face several challenges. People **drain** and build on wetland **habitats**. Some animals are hurt accidentally by fishing nets, cars, and boats.

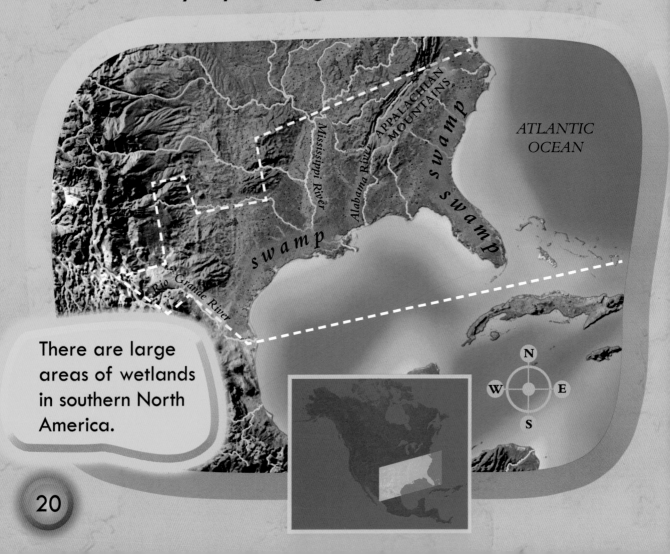

Mississippi River

Alabama River

APPALACHIAN MOUNTAINS

swamp

swamp

swamp

ATLANTIC OCEAN

Rio Grande River

There are large areas of wetlands in southern North America.

N
W E
S

Crocodiles grow new teeth when old ones wear out. They may have 3,000 in a lifetime!

A crocodile's ears, eyes, and nose are on top of its head, so it can spot **prey** while hiding in the water. When prey is close, the crocodile grabs it with its sharp teeth and drags it underwater to drown it.

Gopher frogs stick their eggs to plant stems in ponds. Tadpoles that hatch out of the eggs live and feed in the ponds for three months. In this time, they grow legs and turn into adult frogs.

Adult gopher frogs leave ponds and live on land.

Red wolves live in groups called packs in swamps and forests. Pups are born in dens among plants, in burrows, or in hollow trees. The pack brings the female food so that she can stay with the pups.

All the wolves in a pack help to look after the playful pups!

Mexico

People affect animals in Mexico in different ways. They take water from lakes to drink and to water plants and they take land for building and farming. They bring in new animals that harm the existing Mexican animals.

In Mexico, there are mountains, deserts, forests, and also islands off the coast.

Sonoran Desert

Chihuahuan Desert

SIERRA MADRE MOUNTAINS

Rio Grande River

Chihuahuan forest woodland

forest woodland

PACIFIC OCEAN

Popocatépetl Volcano

N
W   E
S

The raccoon's long nose smells food, and its nimble fingers catch and handle it.

The pygmy raccoon lives only on one island off the coast of Mexico. It hunts crabs and other small **prey** at night. People bring pets to the island that eat raccoons or pass on diseases that kill them.

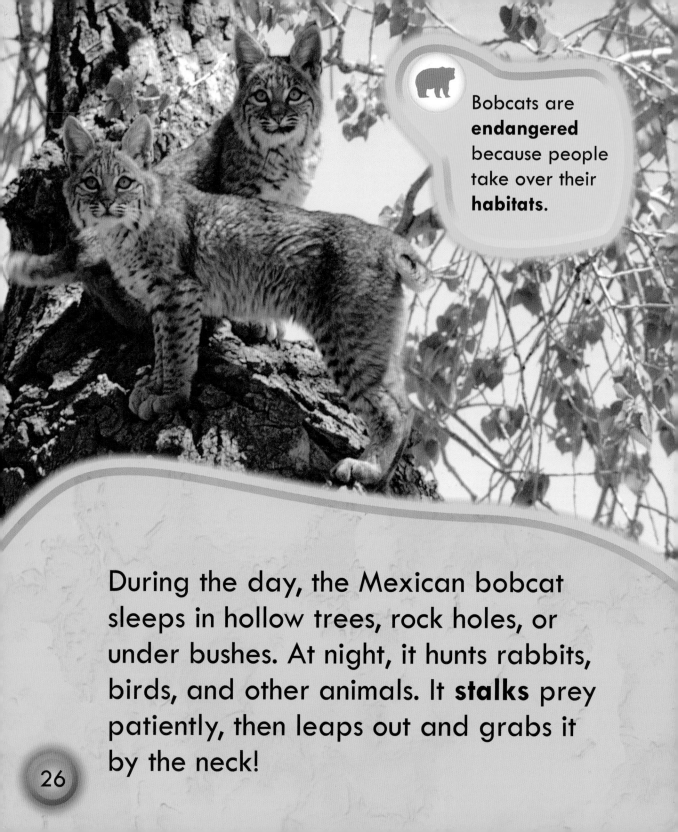

Bobcats are **endangered** because people take over their **habitats.**

During the day, the Mexican bobcat sleeps in hollow trees, rock holes, or under bushes. At night, it hunts rabbits, birds, and other animals. It **stalks** prey patiently, then leaps out and grabs it by the neck!

Axolotls are amphibians that never leave the lakes they were born in. They crawl around eating worms and other small animals. They can regrow almost any part of their body that's injured!

The amazing feathery **gills** on the axolotl's head help it to breathe underwater.

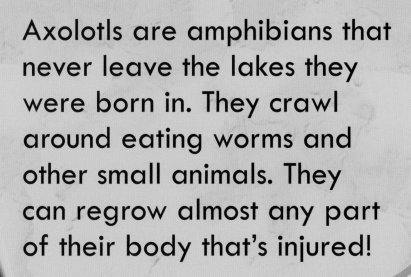

Helping North America's animals

Some countries in North America set up **reserves**. These are places where animals can live safely. The Wood Buffalo National Park protects North America's largest surviving buffalo, or bison, herds.

Without reserves, animals like this bison might die out.

You can help **endangered** animals, too! You could raise money for a group that helps animals, like WWF. You could organize a cake, book, or games sale at school.

Telling other people about endangered animals is one way you can help.

Glossary

alga (the plural is **algae**) plant-like living thing that often grows in water

continent one of seven large areas that make up the world's land

dam barrier that holds back water

desert hot, dry area of land often covered with sand and few plants

drain to cause water to leave something, like a pond

endangered when a type of animal is in danger of dying out

extinct no longer alive; not seen in the wild for 50 years

fin flat body part that sticks out of a fish's body and helps it steer and move

gill body part that animals use to breathe underwater

global warming rise in Earth's temperature, probably caused by human activities such as burning coal

grassland area of land mainly covered in grass

habitat place where plants and animals live

insect small animal with six legs, such as an ant or fly

plain large area of flat land with few trees

prairie large, open area of grassland in America

predator animal that catches and eats other animals

prey animal that gets caught and eaten by other animals

reserve large area of land where plants and animals are protected

scale small, overlapping pieces that cover an animal's body

scrubland hot, dry area of land with bushy plants and sandy soil

stalk to sneak up on

webbed when feet have skin between the toes

wetland land covered in shallow water

Find out more

Books

Endangered Animals (Trailblazers), David Orme (Ransom Publishing, 2009)

North America's Most Amazing Animals (Animal Top Tens), Anita Ganeri (Raintree, 2008)

Internet sites

gowild.wwf.org.uk

Go Wild is the children's club of WWF. You can learn about different animals and their habitats.

www.oum.ox.ac.uk/thezone/animals/extinct/index.htm

Find out about some animals that are now extinct on this website.

Index